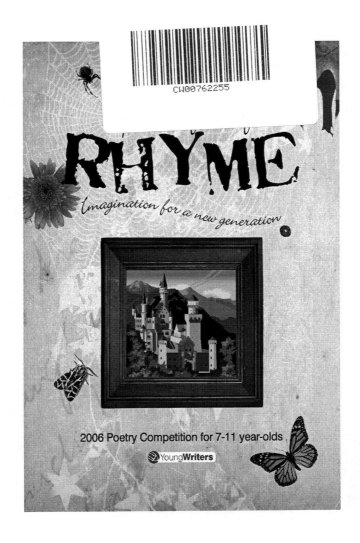

RHYME

Imagination for a new generation

2006 Poetry Competition for 7-11 year-olds

Young**Writers**

Northern England Vol II
Edited by Jessica Woodbridge

 Young**Writers**

First published in Great Britain in 2006 by:
Young Writers
Remus House
Coltsfoot Drive
Peterborough
PE2 9JX
Telephone: 01733 890066
Website: www.youngwriters.co.uk

SB ISBN 1 84602 459 5

Foreword

Young Writers was established in 1991 and has been passionately devoted to the promotion of reading and writing in children and young adults ever since. The quest continues today. Young Writers remains as committed to the nurturing of poetic and literary talent as ever.

This year's Young Writers competition has proven as vibrant and dynamic as ever and we are delighted to present a showcase of the best poetry from across the UK and in some cases overseas. Each poem has been selected from a wealth of *A Pocketful Of Rhyme* entries before ultimately being published in this, our fourteenth primary school poetry series.

Once again, we have been supremely impressed by the overall quality of the entries we have received. The imagination, energy and creativity which has gone into each young writer's entry made choosing the poems a challenging and often difficult but ultimately hugely rewarding task - the general high standard of the work submitted ensured this opportunity to bring their poetry to a larger appreciative audience.

We sincerely hope you are pleased with this final collection and that you will enjoy *A Pocketful Of Rhyme Northern England Vol II* for many years to come.

Contents

Loftus Junior School, Loftus

Maggie Enticknap (9)	39
Connor Hutchinson (9)	40
Tom Limon (8)	41
Shannon Summerson (8)	42
Mileena Vyse (9)	43
Leah-Mae Thompson (9)	44
Elizabeth Cummins (9)	45
Adele Stonehouse (10)	46
James Cocks (10)	47
Sarah Barwick (9)	48
Lauren Foreman (10)	49
Ebony Housam (10)	50
Stacey Bell (9)	51
Lauren Stonehouse (10)	52
Rosie Limon (10)	53
Scott Graham (10)	54
Jessica Walker (10)	55
Robin Gibson (11)	56
Daniel Smithies (10)	57
Dean Hill (10)	58
Chelsea Greenwood (11)	59
Jessica Crutchley (11)	60
William Twaddle (10)	61
Kurtis Pearson (10)	62
Michael Christon (10)	63
Helen Atkinson (11)	64
Hannah Cooper (10)	65
Bethany Simpson (11)	66
Carl Gray (11)	67
Olivia Kemp (11)	68
Scott Thirlwall (10)	69
Cameron Sherred (10)	70
Dan Garbutt (11)	71
Katie Hullah (11)	72
Adam Winspear (11)	73
Ellie Beauchamp (11)	74
Abbie Toshach (10)	75
Jake Peirson (10)	76
Rhys Kemp (10)	77
Nathan Taylor (11)	78
Guy Whitney (11)	79

Dean Stirk (8)   80
Kirsty Thirlwall (9)   81
Paige Yarker (9)   82
Katie Thompson (9)   83
Daniel Ward (9)   84
Tom Tyreman (8)   85
Mason Linford (9)   86
Daniel Jacklin (10)   87

Ludworth Primary School, Ludworth
Marc Lee (11)   88
Anthony Dove (9)   89
Emma Jubb (10)   90
Bobbie Hall (10)   91
Laura Conley (11)   92
Gabrielle Hyland (9)   93
Keiran Lenehan (9)   94
Rachael Woods (8)   95
Matthew Stabler (8)   96
Erin Moyse (9)   97
Lauren Wilson (8)   98
Callum Conley (9)   99
Rachael Waller (8)   100
Kieran Kell (9)   101
Adam Lee (8)   102

Overfields Primary School, Middlesbrough
Andrew Rogers (9)   103
Ellie Pearson (8)   104
Connor Gaunt (9)   105
Grace Weatherall (9)   106
Tommy Young (9)   107
Robbie Livingstone (8)   108
Jessica Hodgson (8)   109
Adele Warrior (7)   110
Daniel McGill (8)   111
Connor Attwood (8)   112
Emily James (8)   113
Liam Clark (7)   114
Martin Marshall-Ellwood (9)   115
Charley Massey (7)   116

Liam Bivens (10)	117
Tiegan Helm (8)	118
Amy Green (10)	119
Jessica Mehnert (10)	120
Amber Sheridan (10)	121
Georgia Cox (11)	122

Robert Ferguson Primary School, Carlisle

Rachel Ramsay (11)	123
Kelsey Davidson (11)	124
Nicola Nunn (10)	125
Bradley Miller (11)	126
Leanne Thomas (11)	127
Samantha Robson (11)	128
Chloe Brown (11)	129
Hannah Gill (10)	130
Steffan James (11)	131
Sally Metcalfe (11)	132
Jenna Selen (10)	133
Adam Martin (11)	134
Bethany Hindmarsh (10)	135
Damian Childs (10)	136
Abbie Turner (10)	137
Lisa Annall (11)	138
Abby Jardine (10)	139
Lauren Little (11)	140

St Paul's RC Primary School, Billingham

Connor Redden (9)	141
Anna Fairs (11)	142
Abigail Noble (10)	143
Andrew Wilson (9)	144
James McCabe (10)	145
Lauriane Povey (10)	146
Jennifer Robinson (10)	147
Joseph Armstrong (9)	148
Hannah McLaren (9)	149
Liam Taylor (10)	150
Ryan Branley (10)	151
Louis Kelly (10)	152
Hope Cain (10)	153

The Poems

Entering A New Life

When I woke up
I opened my wardrobe
And I entered a new world.
It was sprinkled with joy and happiness.
It was like a white wedding and
A white Christmas all on the same day.
But all I wanted to do was get changed.

Nicky Ryan (10)
Greengate Junior School, Barrow-in-Furness

Winter Wonderland

Icy old twigs like an old man's beard.
Crackle, creak go the icy icicles
Lights so bright melting ice and snow.
Drip, drop goes the melting sky above.
Freezing statues, Artic snow, wrap up warm as winter grows.
Cold colours surrounding me *whoosh! whoosh!*
The howling wind speaks, ice glistening in the night.
Wind howling comes forward.

Ellie Mills (11)
Greengate Junior School, Barrow-in-Furness

The Attic

Old and smelly
Big and scary
Silent
Tap, tap, tap
Rats' footsteps
The creepy shadows fade away.

Tyler Godfrey (11)
Greengate Junior School, Barrow-in-Furness

Slowly

Slowly the world is revealed to me,
Ocean by ocean, tree by tree.
I open my eyes and I can see
The world that belongs to me.

Alice Wilmot (10)
Greengate Junior School, Barrow-in-Furness

Etagneergia

Whiteness is flowing everywhere
Sinking into the softness
On a white wedding day
Icicles frozen
Trees bare
Silhouettes following
Echoes and faint voices breaking through
Relaxing and peaceful
Icy breeze blowing against you
Snowballs falling down
Touching the lightness of the ground
A cool wind
Rushes past me
On a winter's night.

Abigail Waite (10)
Greengate Junior School, Barrow-in-Furness

Etagneergia

As I walked through the door
There were spiders everywhere
Everybody carried on, but
Matthew wouldn't dare.

In the attic it was cold
And there was the head of a boar
I looked at all the old things
Wondering what was behind the next door.

In the wonderland it was winter
With icicles hanging off the trees
It was spooky looking around
Wondering what I was going to see.

In the spring it was warm
There were roses in a basket
I imagined people sunbathing
It was fantastic.

Amy Glasgow (11)
Greengate Junior School, Barrow-in-Furness

Winter Wonderland

Icy twigs like an old man's beard,
Icicles falling *drip, drip, drop,*
No colour, only white.

Peaceful as entering the cold modern room,
Fog rising down as fast as lightning
Trees swaying as the trees begin to brighten.
Trees as white as sheep
Drip, drip, drop, as icicles fall.

Kimberley Purcell (11)
Greengate Junior School, Barrow-in-Furness

Winter's Dream

Sparkling winter wonderland
Perfect snowdrift wedding
Icicles, shimmering in the hazy sunlight
Silent, melting breeze
My face feels so cold
As the icy, silver fingertips
Melt away silently,
Tickling my face.

Kirstie Rawlings (11)
Greengate Junior School, Barrow-in-Furness

Etagneergia

In the attic it was dark
Old objects all around,
People looking at different things
And a trunk of clothes on the ground.

In the winter land it was cold
The trees and plants all white
Glittering white icicles scattered off the trees
It was a very snowy sight.

In the garden it was bright
With a hammock hanging up high,
With colourful flowers like summer
And the grass all green with pride.

As I looked around each room
Completely different from the last,
Winter, summer, cold and dark
Some objects from the past.

Natalie Loughran (10)
Greengate Junior School, Barrow-in-Furness

The Future

I am a wizard looking into the future
I see this land will fall
To a demon bear
Strongest above all.

It is an ice demon in the form of a bear
It hides behind leafless trees,
It seems to like this weather
So it can make enemies . . .
Freeze!

It is a deadly bear
Menacingly rampaging through the wood
Someone shoots down the bear
And peace comes to all good.

Jake Day (11)
Greengate Junior School, Barrow-in-Furness

Etagneergia

The attic is dark
Full of modern objects,
Feels cold, smells damp
A man in armour is staring at you.

Through the portal
To the next place
Who knows what we will see.

The crystal garden
As white as snow,
The silky sky falls down on us
We're walking in a wonderland.

Through the portal
To the next room,
Who knows what we will see.

The beautiful garden
Sun gleaming down,
It is springtime
In a warm room.

Through the portal
To the next room,
Back at Greengate
What an adventure.

Samantha Williams (11)
Greengate Junior School, Barrow-in-Furness

Etagneergia

Musky and damp scent haunting you
An old wooden chest, as it opens, it is like a mouse squealing
Cobwebs are hanging off the walls
There are old notes saying,
'If I am not back by the time the leaves have fallen from the trees
Come for me!'

Samara Kendall (11)
Greengate Junior School, Barrow-in-Furness

Winter Wonderland

The evil creature that roams the land
The magical lights that are all around
The twigs that hang over you like a skeleton's hand
The icicles that twirl in the smooth soft breeze
The fortune teller's crystal ball that tells you what you please.

Laura Irving (10)
Greengate Junior School, Barrow-in-Furness

Narnia

As we roam across the dark, black attic
The knight in armour stares at me.

The ice room that is so white, so cold
Has tiny, magic balls lighting as they go.

The bright green garden with flowers growing tall
Has one white hammock rocking in the wind.

I think we're in Narnia.

Alana Storey (11)
Greengate Junior School, Barrow-in-Furness

As White As A Dove

No evil to be seen
It's a magic land,
Soft snowballs glowing
As I hold them in my hand.

No doves to be seen
Their camouflage is feather white,
You cannot see them in the day
But they reveal themselves at night.

Antonia McGuire (11)
Greengate Junior School, Barrow-in-Furness

Winter Wonderland

Whiteness is glowing everywhere
Fur is what you'll need to wear.
Icicles, twigs, snow is falling down
You could have a lovely wedding with a long white gown.
Shadows follow you everywhere
Feel the cool breeze and the night sky air.
Frozen and crunchy
Relaxing and spacious,
I think I need to go to sleep.

Isabelle Roberts (10)
Greengate Junior School, Barrow-in-Furness

White And Calm

White and calm, snow shivering down your spine,
Children getting warm, making no sound.
Bare arms follow you, brown and old,
Old pots on the floor that have never been sold.

White and calm, snow shivering down your spine,
Something watching you making no sound.
It's bare, it's cold, I pull my coat around,
Poor people outside looking for money and pounds.

Francie Martinez (11)
Greengate Junior School, Barrow-in-Furness

Etagneergia

There was an attic
Dark and gloomy that we went through
There were plenty of old things
We touched things too.

We went on through to the second room
And it was filled with new things and old things
Full of beauty and beautiful things we knew.

We went to the third room
Nice and new, we touched things too
It was green and cool.

Kieran Solloway (10)
Greengate Junior School, Barrow-in-Furness

Etagneergia

Past or present you never know
A tin man in an old attic
A teddy bear stuffed with fluff
Etagneergia.

Past or present you never know
Magic balls changing colours
A small elf in this scene.
Etagneergia.

Daniel Smith (10)
Greengate Junior School, Barrow-in-Furness

Etagneergia

At first there was an attic
Full of old stuff and the new
We worked together and looked at things
Just me and you.

We went on through to the second place
Full of beauty and things of grace
It was a winter wonderland
Full of things good and grand.

Into the last room we went
By this time we were all spent
In this room it was summer
And back to the last room we went.

Kieran Smith (11)
Greengate Junior School, Barrow-in-Furness

Etagneergia

Walk in the attic from the past,
Scared and cold,
Twitchy feeling,
Rattling money,
Delicate suitcase.

There it was before my eyes
Winter wonderland,
People watching, even staring,
Gentle feeling,
Rainbow bells.

Walk into a greenhouse,
Fresh flowers,
Smell nice and fresh,
Very clean,
That's Etagneergia.

Shannon Leith (10)
Greengate Junior School, Barrow-in-Furness

The Creepy Entrance

Cold and old,
Damp and unwanted,
Silent,
Creatures all around,
As the mysterious man walks through.

Toni Turnbull (10)
Greengate Junior School, Barrow-in-Furness

Shivery Mountain

Ice taking breath away
Coldness within light.
The fearsome beast attacks us
The little beast creeps up behind.

A shiver runs down my spine
Evil always returns
No one ever forgets it
Why do people feel cursed
In dark and shivery places?

On a shivery mountain
One spike of coldness
And you're gone forever
There is no place to escape.

Arron Instance (10)
Greengate Junior School, Barrow-in-Furness

Scary Night

It's dark and scary
Quiet and shivery
With spiders hairy and long
Spiderwebs sticky everywhere
With things that crawl and things that bite
I shiver all night.

Jordan Clarke (10)
Greengate Junior School, Barrow-in-Furness

The Attic

I am a dark dusty place
With cockroaches scuttling round
My feet and up my legs,
There are hairy spiders in my hair.
Please help me, I'm scared!

Danny Hoyland (11)
Greengate Junior School, Barrow-in-Furness

The Attic

In a dark and dusty attic
On the walls I can see dead sea horses and deer heads
Red-backed spiders creeping up my back
Something touched me, what was it?

Paul Martindale (10)
Greengate Junior School, Barrow-in-Furness

Lost!

In a winter land all cold with frost,
My heart beats wild as the icy light captures me in its cold hands.
Lost in the white heaven of hope
Like an ice cube trying to release coldness into freedom
Floundering in the frost
How to get out I do not know,
I'm lost!

Hayley Jackson (10)
Greengate Junior School, Barrow-in-Furness

White Life

The silver beast that strolls through the snow
The cold breeze that freezes the white lonely trees
The sky is as white as snowflakes
The beast is ready to strike.

Josh Yeo (11)
Greengate Junior School, Barrow-in-Furness

What's That There?

It was freezing and cloudy
Sleepy fields of white.
It looks like Christmas all around,
An animal couldn't live on that ground.
What is that crawling there?
Creepy-crawlies strip it bare.

Craig Anderson (11)
Greengate Junior School, Barrow-in-Furness

The Past

The place is quiet
The past has come back,
The old wedding clothes awaken
It is like the world starting again.
Umbrellas made in China
Old kettles boiling again.

The black and white pictures
On the mantelpiece where they used to be,
Old frames and crinkled pictures
I think the past can teach us a lot.

Paige O'Brien (10)
Greengate Junior School, Barrow-in-Furness

Winter World

Sprinkles of snow cover the ground
Quiet, hush all around
Icicles hanging from winter trees
Swaying in the gentle breeze.

Josh Purcell (11)
Greengate Junior School, Barrow-in-Furness

Nardia

Smells old
Relaxed, clam
Makes you want to rummage
Through and through
Makes you want to sleep
All day long
A blast from the past.

Mica Stitt (10)
Greengate Junior School, Barrow-in-Furness

Etagneergia

One last night in a spooky place
Get away from spiders and horrid smells,
Walk to a peaceful forest of snow
Walk on crunchy leaves and icicles
Then you come to a spring garden
Full of colour and light
This is a beautiful day.

Atarah Beach (10)
Greengate Junior School, Barrow-in-Furness

Etagneergia

Cold and damp
Dark and gloomy
Abandoned and unwanted
Silent but loud
Creepy and unnerving.

Beth Clarke (10)
Greengate Junior School, Barrow-in-Furness

Etagneergia

Going through the portal, spiders everywhere
Everybody went through,
But Matthew wouldn't dare.
We went into the attic, winterland and spring.

In the attic
It was cold,
Books, trunks and candleholders sitting there,
All cold and bare covered in dust.

In winterland my favourite place to be
All silent, cold and white,
It felt all Christmassy once again
So peaceful and so chilly.

In the garden
All green and summery
Picked roses all white and snowy
Picnic placed on the floor.

Charlotte Dawson (10)
Greengate Junior School, Barrow-in-Furness

Etagneergia

Going through the portal, insects everywhere
Everybody went through but Matthew wouldn't dare.
We went to the attic, winterland and spring
And saw a bear with wings.
We went through the portal again and again
And arrived back home
After a good journey to different places.

Matthew Burnett (10)
Greengate Junior School, Barrow-in-Furness

As I Go In What Do I See?

As I go in, what do I see?
I see a crystal ball, glowing like a sunset.

As I go in, what do I see?
I see a hammock, hanging high.

As I go in, what do I see?
I see a knight standing tall.

As I go in, what do I see?
I see spiders hanging tall.

As I go in, what do I see?
Everything, bye-bye.

Chloe Martin (10)
Greengate Junior School, Barrow-in-Furness

Etagneergia - Cinquains

Winter
Winter
Magic weather
Icicles in the trees
Winter trees, Christmas on its way
Snow cave.

Summer
Flowers
Tasty picnic
Warm sun, trees and flowers
Safe fantasy, picnic on grass
Summer.

Attic
Attic
Fancy dress box
Umbrella from the past
Delicate object from the past
Candles.

Sarah Adams (10)
Greengate Junior School, Barrow-in-Furness

School

Mum says . . . school is for learning
School is for education
History, literacy, sharing
Learning to write and read.

But I say . . . school is for fun
And seeing our friends
Doing art and playing games
And playing sports
Let's all go to school.

Maggie Enticknap (9)
Loftus Junior School, Loftus

Football

My mother says football's crazy,
Football's daft,
Football's crackers,
I like craft,
You have to wait for the ball,
I'd rather go to the mall,
You get stains on your shorts
I'd rather go to court.

But I say football's class,
Football's good,
I'd do anything to go to a class,
Football's lovely,
Football's great,
Football's amazing for my best mate.

Connor Hutchinson (9)
Loftus Junior School, Loftus

Look Out There's A Wave About

Last summer I went canoeing
I jumped out and started swimming.

I got back in
That was the end of my swim.

Right behind me, there was a big wave
No running away for me, because I was so brave.

I got back on to the beach
I ate a little peach.
Then I went home
And I didn't moan.

Tom Limon (8)
Loftus Junior School, Loftus

School

My mum says that you should go to school to learn,
It is good fun, says my mum
To do maths, literacy, science, geography, history and mental maths,
says my mum.
I say that yes, school is good fun
But sometimes you get shouted at,
Yes I know you go to school to learn,
Sometimes it can be fun but sometimes it can be boring.
That's what I say.

Shannon Summerson (8)
Loftus Junior School, Loftus

The Colours Of The Rainbow

Red is the first colour in the rainbow,
What a pretty colour it is,
It is the same colour as blood.
Orange is the second colour in the rainbow,
What a beautiful colour it is,
It reminds me of the fruit.
Yellow is the third colour of the rainbow,
What a lovely colour it is,
It is the same colour as the sun.
Green is the fourth colour of the rainbow,
What a wonderful colour it is,
It reminds me of the fresh grass.
Blue is the fifth colour of the rainbow,
What a great colour it is,
Blue reminds us of the sky.
Indigo is the sixth colour of the rainbow,
What a strange colour it is,
It is a very calming colour.
Purple is the seventh colour of the rainbow,
What a bright colour it is,
Royal kings dress in this colour
And now we are at the end of the rainbow.

Mileena Vyse (9)
Loftus Junior School, Loftus

Riddle

Animal with eight legs
Holding a scarf
Stripes on each leg
Hat is blue and it has a yellow sort of a smile
It has black googly eyes.

Leah-Mae Thompson (9)
Loftus Junior School, Loftus

Riddle

It's long and straight
It gets cut by a lawnmower
It gets cut every month
You put it in your garden
It grows and grows
And some animals eat it.

Elizabeth Cummins (9)
Loftus Junior School, Loftus

Our Brain

Our brainstem keeps us alive
Wake ya self up and have a jive.

It's Monday morning, we're all asleep
When we started work I just had to peep.

Left side, right side, they're all dreaming
My teachers shouted, 'Please start reading!'

This morning I was awake
Outside I just had to shake.

This morning my brain was very controlling
This morning my brain was rock and rolling.

On a Monday my brain's a bit slack
As the week goes on it starts to crack.

As the week goes by my brain is tingling
As the day goes on my brain is zinging.

School's just finished, my brain's resting
When I get home my mum starts testing.

Adele Stonehouse (10)
Loftus Junior School, Loftus

Our Brain

Our brains are lousy on Monday morning,
They need to get creative,
They need to get buzzing and tinging to the beat.

Our brains are amazing,
Our brains are controlling,
Our brains are dreaming about
Movement, pictures, music.

James Cocks (10)
Loftus Junior School, Loftus

My Brain

Pictures movement, colour to the brain is awesome, just like you.

Sleepy, empty, over tired, sluggish, lazy, really lousy,
Also feeling very drowsy.

Now the brain is buzzing with excitement,
Amazing, no more gazing cos we're awake.

Time to prepare a speech about the amazing leech.

Work is done, school is over,
Now it's time to go and play for the rest of the day.

Sarah Barwick (9)
Loftus Junior School, Loftus

Jolly Blue Giant

The blue's the biggest kind of whale
At thirty metres long, top to tail.
The largest creature on the Earth,
It's seven metres long at birth.
It glides through the water to catch its prey,
If you should meet one face to face
You should not run away a pace.
It's not that blue whales are wimps
It's just that all they eat is shrimps!

Lauren Foreman (10)
Loftus Junior School, Loftus

About Our Brains

On a Monday morning our brains are very lazy, lousy and sluggish
We need to be awake.
As the day goes on,
Our brains become awake, happy and creative.
I do brain gym to help my brain come alive.
Then my teacher screams, 'Are you awake?'
We shout, 'Yes Miss, let's start work!'
Then we do numeracy, literacy, science and history.
The bell rings, let's go home
We go home, watch telly then sleep.
Then it all starts over again.

Ebony Housam (10)
Loftus Junior School, Loftus

Our Brain

Monday morning our brains are sluggish, dormant and lazy
People falling asleep.
'Cross crawl,' someone shouts, there's a loud screech of chairs.
Our brain becomes buzzing, excited and our brain becomes alive.
Left side and right side responding.
Left side starting to read and write, looking carefully.
Right side uses imagination, dancing, playing.
Our corpus collosum is a bridge and is connected.
What's happened?
The corpus collosum has broken and the brain stem is taking over.
Who knows what's going to happen!

Stacey Bell (9)
Loftus Junior School, Loftus

The Brain

The brain is happy, the brain is sad,
The brain is cracking, the brain is mad.

The brain is lousy, the brain is drowsy,
The brain is tingling, the brain is zinging.

The brain is creating, the brain is buzzing,
The brain is reading, the brain is writing.

The brain is amazing, the brain is excited,
The brain is dreaming, the brain is breathing.

The brain likes music, the brain likes movement,
The brain likes colours, the brain likes pictures.

Lauren Stonehouse (10)
Loftus Junior School, Loftus

My Nightmare

I lay fast asleep in bed
With a nightmare going through my head.
Running through the dark night
Hoping to find a street light.
Then what do I hear?
The patter of feet loud and clear.
I turned around to see
A huge green monster chasing me.
Great big claws and arms so long
Ghastly breath it smelt so strong.
Massive eyes they stared at me
It was easy to tell I was his tea!
Suddenly I woke with a fright
What a relief it was no longer night.

Rosie Limon (10)
Loftus Junior School, Loftus

Sadness

Sadness is brown,
Brown like the damp earth's floor.
Sadness tastes like old water
Stagnant on a marsh.
Sadness smells like smoke,
Smoke from a house fire.
Sadness feels like the cold steel of a blade,
Reopening a wound.
Sadness looks like the glowing eyes of a mercenary,
Not wanting to kill.
Sadness reminds me of the sight of a grave
Bringing old memories to pass.
Sadness sounds like crunching paper
Flattened on the floor.
Sadness.

Scott Graham (10)
Loftus Junior School, Loftus

Happiness

Happiness is light blue like the light blue sky.
Happiness smells like a flower blooming happily.
Happiness looks like a fizzy drink in the summer heat.
Happiness tastes like a cornet dribbling down my finger.
Happiness feels like the warm butter slipping down my chin.
Happiness sounds like a drum repeating.
Happiness reminds me of my first ice cream rushing down my throat.
Happiness.

Jessica Walker (10)
Loftus Junior School, Loftus

Sadness

Sadness is blue,
Blue like the tears of fear.
Sadness looks like the devil,
The devil that rages through me.
Sadness reminds me of the dead,
The dead that we loved, who died for no reason.
Sadness sounds like a scream,
A scream of the dead that now rests in peace.
Sadness tastes of cheese,
The cheese that's mouldy and crumbles in your mouth.
Sadness smells like ash,
Ash of bodies that have burnt at cremations.
Sadness feels like smoothness
But it is not what you expected to feel.
Sadness, sadness, sadness.

Robin Gibson (11)
Loftus Junior School, Loftus

Happiness

Happiness is blue, blue like a clear blue sky.
Happiness tastes like a gorgeous strawberry sweet slipping down
                                                    your throat.
Happiness feels like a person being tickled till he can't laugh any more.
Happiness sounds like children laughing, going down a roller coaster.
Happiness reminds me of when I scored my first goal in football.
Happiness smells like a gorgeous strawberry just fresh out
                                                    of a garden.
Happiness looks like a shooting star speeding through the sky.
Happiness.

Daniel Smithies (10)
Loftus Junior School, Loftus

Happiness

Happiness is orange, orange like the flame of a birthday candle.
Happiness feels like going on holiday for the first time.
Happiness sounds like a cheer of joy all around me.
Happiness reminds me of Christmas time opening presents.
Happiness smells like chicken korma, cooking away.
Happiness looks like your favourite football team winning a match.
Happiness tastes like a cup of tea when you're in the mood.
Happiness, happiness, happiness,
This is happiness.

Dean Hill (10)
Loftus Junior School, Loftus

Hate

Hate is black, black like a poisoned apple.
Hate.
Hate smells like a litre of sour milk.
Hate.
Hate sounds like a raging bull in the windy marsh.
Hate.
Hate looks like a splattered paint factory.
Hate.
Hate tastes like burnt biscuits.
Hate.
Hate feels like a scalding pot of tea.
Hate.
Hate reminds me of somebody skimming stones.
Hate.
Hate is a strong emotion.
Hate!

Chelsea Greenwood (11)
Loftus Junior School, Loftus

Hate

Hate is purple, purple like a painful black eye.
Hate.
Hate sounds like a cry of a boy in dreadful pain.
Hate.
Hate tastes like a sour carton of milk.
Hate.
Hate feels like the rough sea crashing against your feet.
Hate.
Hate reminds me of the black night sky being filled with fireworks.
Hate.
Hate smells like a fiery burnt piece of toast.
Hate.
Hate looks like a squealing boar raging through the woods.
Hate.
Hate is purple, purple like a painful black eye.
Hate.

Jessica Crutchley (11)
Loftus Junior School, Loftus

Hate

Hate is red like a flaming fire.
Hate.
Hate tastes like a sour apple.
Hate.
Hate feels like a punch in the face.
Hate.
Hate reminds me of slamming doors.
Hate.
Hate smells like super sharp cheese.
Hate.
Hate looks like a big bulldozer.
Hate.
Hate sound like a baby squealing.
Hate.
Hate is red.

William Twaddle (10)
Loftus Junior School, Loftus

Happiness

Happiness is red.
Happiness is like a big red smile.
Happiness sounds like laughter.
Happiness is like the laughter of children in a school playground.
Happiness reminds me of a big happy smile.
Happiness is like a child's face on Christmas Day.
Happiness smells like a freshly cooked burger.
Happiness is like a freshly cooked burger just from the oven.
Happiness looks like a love heart.
Happiness is like a love heart on a Valentine's Day card.
Happiness tastes like fish and chips.
Happiness is like greasy fish and chips for my dinner.
Happiness feels like opening a present.
Happiness is like opening a Christmas present you have wanted
                                                    all year round.
Happiness.
Happiness.
Happiness.

Kurtis Pearson (10)
Loftus Junior School, Loftus

Fun

Fun is blue, blue like the blue summer's sky.
Fun.
Fun reminds me of a whizzing roller coaster.
Fun.
Fun feels like snow blowing in my face.
Fun.
Fun looks like someone splashing and playing in the sea.
Fun.
Fun tastes like a lemon topped ice cream.
Fun.
Fun sounds like a seagull swooping down at a fish in the sea.
Fun.
Fun smells like some chocolate melting in the sun.
Fun, fun, fun.

Michael Christon (10)
Loftus Junior School, Loftus

Sadness

Sadness is pink, pink like a fuchsia dying.
Sadness sounds like funeral bells ringing at the church.
Sadness tastes like sour chews that leave a long, lasting sting.
Sadness smells like raw onions causing watery eyes.
Sadness feels like gum stuck to your shoe that will never come off.
Sadness looks like fungi spreading across the grass.
Sadness reminds me of my great grandad, old and remembered.

Helen Atkinson (11)
Loftus Junior School, Loftus

Sadness

Sadness is blue, blue like a running tap.
Sadness.
Sadness smells like bacon, bacon sizzling in a pan.
Sadness.
Sadness feels like a snowball, a snowball hitting your face.
Sadness.
Sadness looks like condensation that trickles down a window.
Sadness.
Sadness reminds me of an onion that makes you cry.
Sadness.
Sadness sounds like a baby, a baby weeping in its sleep.
Sadness.
Sadness tastes like tinned tomatoes when the juice runs down your
throat.
Sadness.

Hannah Cooper (10)
Loftus Junior School, Loftus

Happiness

Happiness is orange, orange like the shining summer sun.
Happiness.
Happiness reminds me of the first day of spring.
Happiness.
Happiness smells like fresh orange juice in the morning.
Happiness.
Happiness looks like children running across the sunset beach.
Happiness.
Happiness tastes like a lovely buttered crumpet before school.
Happiness.
Happiness feels like a bear hug from my mum before I go to sleep.
Happiness.
Happiness sounds like a sweet tune from a trumpet in the distance.
Happiness.
Happiness is orange, orange like the shining summer sun.
Happiness is our friend.

Bethany Simpson (11)
Loftus Junior School, Loftus

Fun

Fun tastes like sweets you've just eaten and you want some more.
It sounds like children laughing and having fun.
It feels like someone is tickling you.
Fun reminds you of happy times with your family.
It looks like people enjoying themselves on the beach building sandcastles.
Fun smells like chocolate just being melted.

Carl Gray (11)
Loftus Junior School, Loftus

Anger

What does it sound like?
It sounds like a very loud scary voice!
What does it look like?
It looks like a bright red face!
What does it feel like?
It feels like my heart is going to explode!
What does it remind you of?
It reminds me of something on fire!
What does it smell like?
It smells like a volcano!
What does it taste like?
It tastes like burning steel!

Olivia Kemp (11)
Loftus Junior School, Loftus

Darkness

The colour of darkness is dark and grey.
It looks like the Grim Reaper fading away.
Darkness sounds like the echoing of a dome.
It feels like you're all alone.
Darkness smells of soup that's cold.
It tastes like a rotten cold drink.
The darkness reminds me of my worst nightmare ever.

Scott Thirlwall (10)
Loftus Junior School, Loftus

Darkness

What does it feel like?
It feels like a ghost in every direction.
What does it remind me of?
It reminds me of fireworks going off.
What does it taste like?
It tastes like raw meat just out of the freezer.
What does it sound like?
Darkness sounds like an old woman screaming for mercy.
What does it look like?
Darkness looks like a black creature on the wall and it won't come off.
What colour is it?
Darkness is black with red blood lines on it.

Cameron Sherred (10)
Loftus Junior School, Loftus

Hunger

It tastes like the unhealthy bitter emptiness of waiting to eat.
It looks like a buffet fit for a king slowly vanishing.
It reminds me of the time I last ate.
It sounds like a starving tribe desperately screaming for food.
It feels like a foul hairy beast growling for food.
It smells like succulent bacon being drawn away from you.

Dan Garbutt (11)
Loftus Junior School, Loftus

Happiness

Happiness tastes like ice cream dripping all over your mouth.
It smells like popcorn just being warmed up in the microwave.
Happiness sounds like children laughing for fun.
It looks like adults smiling at you and never stopping.
Happiness reminds me of babies shouting for fun.
It feels like someone cuddling you for laughter.
Happiness is pale pink like a butterfly's wing.

Katie Hullah (11)
Loftus Junior School, Loftus

Hunger

Hunger is like a dark green chameleon.
It looks like hallucinations of food.
Hunger feels like hunger pangs in your stomach.
It smells like the food you love like curry.
Hunger reminds me of a dream when I could have what I want to eat.
It sounds like a troll hitting your belly with a club.
Hunger tastes like a double pepperoni pizza.

Adam Winspear (11)
Loftus Junior School, Loftus

Happiness

It smells like the helium in a balloon,
While it's floating up in the sky.
It tastes like the icing on a freshly baked cake
While you're putting it into your mouth.
It sounds like the laughter of a group of young children
While playing so nicely on the beach.
It feels like the comfort of your bed at night
While you're tucking yourself tightly in.
It looks like the ticks and the very high scores on a test
While you're checking your marks.
It reminds me of the thought of the summer holidays
In the very last hour of school.
What is the colour of happiness?
It is the colour of yellow, a bright shining sun and the newly born
                                chicks in the spring.

Ellie Beauchamp (11)
Loftus Junior School, Loftus

Anger

What does it look like?
It looks like you've just stepped in a puddle and you're drenched
to the floor.
What does it feel like?
It feels like wanting to hit someone for no reason at all.
What does it sound like?
It sounds like a squeaking floorboard that moans every day.
What does it taste like?
It tastes like rotten eggs sat in a bin.
What does it remind me of?
It reminds me of people screaming and shouting.

Abbie Toshach (10)
Loftus Junior School, Loftus

Darkness

What colour is it?
The colour is midnight black.
What does it look like?
It looks like the Grim Reaper, going up in flames.
What does it sound like?
It sounds like a strange *whoa* in the woods.
What does it smell like?
It smells like logs burning on a fire.
What does it remind me of?
It reminds me of bats flying swiftly in the sky.
What does it taste like?
It tastes like seawater when you swallow it.

Jake Peirson (10)
Loftus Junior School, Loftus

Darkness

It looks like shadows creeping around.
Darkness sounds like noises from behind you.
It feels like you're lonely with no one to see or hear.
Darkness tastes like bitter black coffee.
It smells like a damp, cold cellar.
Darkness reminds me of the black robes
The Grim Reaper wears to take people's lives away.

Rhys Kemp (10)
Loftus Junior School, Loftus

Anger

What does it feel like?
It feels like you want a fight.

What does it look like?
It looks like Boro, getting knocked out of the Carling Cup.

What does it taste like?
It tastes like strong blood.

What colour is it?
It is the colour of a bat someone has been hit with.

Nathan Taylor (11)
Loftus Junior School, Loftus

Fun

What does it taste like?
It tastes like popcorn, melting in your mouth.

What does it sound like?
It sounds like someone skipping through a field with roses.

What does it feel like?
It feels like being warm and cosy when you are tucked up in bed.

What does it look like?
It looks like a butterfly fluttering around you.

What does it smell like?
It smells like Butterkist popcorn warmed up in the microwave
And melted with butter and sugar.

Guy Whitney (11)
Loftus Junior School, Loftus

Viking War Song

Go to war
Shiny swords
Chopped to pieces
Many get killed
Dragon-headed ships
Big wooden catapults
Jewelled swords
Hammer headed axes.

Dean Stirk (8)
Loftus Junior School, Loftus

Odin

Lived in Valhalla.
City to the gods.
Son called Balder.
Married to Frigg.
Blood brother Loki.
Frightened people
With his bow.
Mightiest God,
Travelled to realms
In the Nordic world.
Magical God.
Magical wisdom.
Strictly mental.
Polarized God.

Kirsty Thirlwall (9)
Loftus Junior School, Loftus

Vikings

Weapons.
They had shiny swords.
Very sharp spears.
They had small daggers.
They had sharp axes.
The axes had blood on.
They chopped people's heads off.
They took away the women.
They stole the money.
They smuggled all the gold.
Men went to battle.
Many got killed.
They sailed away in long boats.
They killed all the people.

Paige Yarker (9)
Loftus Junior School, Loftus

Vikings

Men got killed
They were rich
Scandinavia
They had axes
Left their homes
Lived in Denmark
Lived in Sweden
Lived in Norway
They stole food
They stole women
They stole money
Settled in Britain
Sailed in long boats
No horns on helmets
They went conquering
Went to war
Lived on farms
In the middle of our country.

Katie Thompson (9)
Loftus Junior School, Loftus

Viking Rules

Lived in Sweden
Lived in Denmark
Lived in Norway
They had swords
And heavy axes
Sharp spears
Bows and arrows
Off they go
Fighting everywhere
Everyone
Shot to pieces
Lots of blood
No horns!
They stole the women
Money and food
They killed the Saxons
More and more
They went to war
Left their homes
Lived on farms
Into the middle of the country
Here come the Vikings.

Daniel Ward (9)
Loftus Junior School, Loftus

The Viking Storm

Sharp swords
Powerful axes
Shining spears
Roundy shields
Lived in Norway
Lived in Denmark
Lived in Sweden
Thatched cottages
Burning down
They set sail
Killing people
Everywhere they went
They used long ships
Dragon-headed.

Tom Tyreman (8)
Loftus Junior School, Loftus

Odin

Married to a beautiful God
Called Frigg.
He had a child
Named Balder.
Blood brother to trickster Loki.
Full of mischief.
His bow was fierce
Frightening people away.
His spear was powerful
Called Grungir.
Valhalla was his home.
Upon a horse with eight legs he rode
And it was called Sleipher.

Mason Linford (9)
Loftus Junior School, Loftus

Fun

Fun is a rainbow.
Rainbow is like a warm day with the rainbow out.
Fun tastes like chicken nuggets and chips.
Fun looks like a big hairy ape.
Fun sounds like children playing in the park.
Fun smells like chocolate cake and custard.
Fun reminds me of going to the movies.
Fun feels like a board game.
Fun is a rainbow, with a rainbow out in the sun.

Daniel Jacklin (10)
Loftus Junior School, Loftus

The Highwayman

(Inspired by 'The Highwayman' by Alfred Noyes)

Highwayman shall come riding, riding, riding
He shall come riding up to the old inn door.

Intelligent as he may be, he gave away his plan,
To accompany Bess his one true love.

Gorgeous he was, lace at his chin and breeches of brown doe skin
A coat of the claret velvet, the claret velvet.

His pistol butt's a twinkle engraved with gold and jewels
(Ruby, sapphire and emeralds)
Which twinkled, yes twinkled, under the starlit sky.

Wondrous he looked with his jewel encrusted pistol
And his twinkling rapier, he was like a sparkling diamond.

Alarmed he was when his heart's desire, his one true love
Had shot herself, shot herself to warn him
That the soldiers had started the search party.

Young and good looking he was
But his charm did not satisfy the resentfulness of the soldiers.

Masked and nameless to all, he was once unknown and quiet
Because he would be found and shot down, down, like a dog.

Apoplectic he was, shouting a curse to the sky and rapidly swinging
his rapier up high.

Nevertheless, they say the highwayman was dead
But he was dead, but his love was not!

Marc Lee (11)
Ludworth Primary School, Ludworth

Bess

(Inspired by 'The Highwayman' by Alfred Noyes)

B eautiful Bess awaits her love.
E ndless waiting for Bess as the highwayman comes riding,
                                        riding, riding.
S tanding helpless, she is hoping with a gun pointed to her heart.
S ad Bess died in the moonlight drenched in blood in the moonlight.

Anthony Dove (9)
Ludworth Primary School, Ludworth

What Am I?

Allow me to describe myself
I live upon a dusty shelf
I get bought for sixty-pence
Then I get put in a pan . . . they fry me
So can you guess what I am?
Don't be mean because you know . . .
I am a tin of *baked beans!*

Emma Jubb (10)
Ludworth Primary School, Ludworth

Bess

(Inspired by 'The Highwayman' by Alfred Noyes)

B ack he came as he said he would, waiting for him was Bess.
   He heard the gunshot and turned away.
E legant, he rode away into the moonlight, he galloped away.
S he looked like a rag doll, dead, hanging in the moonlight.
S elf sacrificed her life for her true love, the highwayman!

Bobbie Hall (10)
Ludworth Primary School, Ludworth

The Highwayman
(Inspired by 'The Highwayman' by Alfred Noyes)

H andsome young man dressed in the best.
I ntelligent or so the landlord's daughter,
    Yes, the landlord's black-eyed daughter, Bess thought.
G reat ride, more rapid than the scarlet redcoats.
H e was the dead man that said,
'W atch for me by moonlight, look for me by moonlight.
    I'll come to thee by moonlight through hell should bar the way.'
    With the redcoats hurrying him throughout the day.
A s it occurred to him Bess had looked for him by moonlight,
    Watched for him by moonlight, he trotted away.
Y ounger than the moonlit sky Bess and the highwayman's love
    Shall never die.
M ean as a wolf he cursed the moonlit sky.
A s for Bess, the young girl, when she died it killed
    The highwayman's world.
N ow on a winter's night,
    The highwayman comes riding, riding,
    The highwayman comes riding up to the old inn door!

Laura Conley (11)
Ludworth Primary School, Ludworth

Magical World

I see unicorns in the sky
They are way up high
Wizards making potions with lizards
Hearing the sound of the magical underground
What a sight
Of that bright light
Shooting stars shimmering everywhere
Birds are singing in the air
This is what makes a magical world.

Gabrielle Hyland (9)
Ludworth Primary School, Ludworth

Stars

Christmas is magical
The sparkly snowflakes fall to the ground
Stars twinkle up above
I feel that they are looking down.

Keiran Lenehan (9)
Ludworth Primary School, Ludworth

Mysterious Tricks

Tricks, tricks in the sky
Whizzing round, as magic goes by.
Witches, witches flying high
On their strong broomsticks in the sky.
Magical stars shining bright
Twinkling brightly in the night.

Rachael Woods (8)
Ludworth Primary School, Ludworth

Winter Magic

Christmas is magic
Christmas is fun
Dropping snowflakes
Twinkle to the ground
Smiling faces all around.

Animals hide away from the cold
The magical winter is here
The animals are warm
They hide away from the storm.

Matthew Stabler (8)
Ludworth Primary School, Ludworth

Colourful Magic

Magic things are all around
Magic things are in the town
Lights are flickering in the night
You'd better watch out or you will get a fright.

Witches waving magical wands over their cauldrons
Magic potions, colourful vortexes
Whirl round and round, listen closely
You may hear the awful sound.

Erin Moyse (9)
Ludworth Primary School, Ludworth

Starry Dreams

Dreams, dreams, floating to the ground
Dreams, dreams when I sleep
Magical dreams are all around
Dreams of pink fairies dancing around
I love my magical dreams.

Shooting stars in the air
Shooting stars are everywhere
Shooting stars are really bright
Magical stars in the night.

Lauren Wilson (8)
Ludworth Primary School, Ludworth

Can You Feel The Magic?

Magic is fun
Magic is hard
Magic is the thing in my heart.

Magic, magic all around
Magic, magic on the ground
Magic, magic in the air
All the magic in the world to share.

Callum Conley (9)
Ludworth Primary School, Ludworth

I Love To Dream

Sparkly spells
Twinkly stars
Can you see all the magic floating around?

I love to dream every night
Of fairies, parties and all things nice
Magical dreams are in the air
They make me feel like I'm really there.

Rachael Waller (8)
Ludworth Primary School, Ludworth

Magical Wizards

Magic is good
Magic is fun
Magic is all around us
So, come and join the fun.

Big black bats and purple hats
Wizards floating in the air
Spells are bubbling everywhere.

Kieran Kell (9)
Ludworth Primary School, Ludworth

Christmas Time

Snowflakes, snowflakes all around
Snowflakes, snowflakes, float softly to the ground.
All the snowflakes in the air
Floating around in the clear fresh air.

Animals at Christmas hide under the ground,
It's too cold for them to run around.
Magical snowflakes floating down
It's like a white blanket covering the ground.

Adam Lee (8)
Ludworth Primary School, Ludworth

Out Of My Window

A house in the distance,
A bin it is, green and brown,
A car and a bird,
A tree swaying in the breeze,
The wind is blowing like a baby tornado,
A snail sliding across my window sill,
A worm under the ground,
A bird falls from the sky,
Sad because a dog got run over.
Who made the sky?

Andrew Rogers (9)
Overfields Primary School, Middlesbrough

My View From A Window

Eston Hills in the distance.
A house, the colour of white.
Birds singing and my dogs barking,
All of the birds and trees move with the wind.
Snow is coming down like sprinkling salt and it is coming down fast.
All of my dogs are barking at each other,
All of the dogs are growling at each other because they are fighting
all the time.
I can see the weather changing all the time, falling rain.
I like seeing all of the animals playing with each other.
It is going to rain.
I can see rain.
People are talking to me all the time.

Ellie Pearson (8)
Overfields Primary School, Middlesbrough

Hedgehog

Call me spiky brown.
I live in hedges and bushes because it is shady.
You can call me pencil sharpener because my spikes are like razors.
I have been awake all night because I am nocturnal.
I spend my time scavenging for snacks.
Snails, spiders and bugs make my mouth water and
                                        my tummy content.
When a predator comes I roll into a tight ball.
Prickles are my armour but nothing can protect me from
                                        a metal monster.
Then I am a flattened piece of meat.

Connor Gaunt (9)
Overfields Primary School, Middlesbrough

Crocodile

Green grinder,
Camouflaged killer
Heavy hider
River lover
Flesh tearer
Long snapper
What am I?

Grace Weatherall (9)
Overfields Primary School, Middlesbrough

My View

Trees up the hills
Fresh green wavy grass.
The wind wrapping its arms around the house.
Noisy drilling from the builders.
Birds swooping down after worms.
It's a dark, gloomy slow day,
With fog surrounding the trees.
I see my old dog fluffy chasing after birds.
The eagle is singing and it echoes through the house.
I feel bored and frozen.
Is it going to be OK?
Of course, it's going to be alright.
A woodlouse crawls on my window.

Tommy Young (9)
Overfields Primary School, Middlesbrough

Out Of My Window

Through my bedroom window I see bushes and trees.
Close to me I see marks, shady and grey.
I hear cars trampling on the road.
I hear trees rattling on mountains.
I see birds flapping wings gently.
Rain pours down and splashes rapidly.
I hear cats purring slowly.
I hear dogs barking but I can't see anything.
Cars just appear from the road.
When it's raining I feel dull.
I don't know how things just grow.
I ask Mum lots of questions about nature.
I hear things falling and they get my attention.

Robbie Livingstone (8)
Overfields Primary School, Middlesbrough

Dog Began

(Based on 'Cat Began' by Andrew Matthews)

He took the crashing waves
And made his voice.
He took a razorblade
And made his teeth.
He took the smooth dove
And made his coat.
He took the wiggly lion
And made his movement
And Dog was made.

Jessica Hodgson (8)
Overfields Primary School, Middlesbrough

Ladybird

I can't survive the cold.
I live in the wind.
I think I should have spots to look delightful
And I think other animals should have wings as well.
I glide across the sky and the air cools me off.

Adele Warrior (7)
Overfields Primary School, Middlesbrough

Call Me Dog McGill

My name is Dog McGill
I am good at chasing cats.
I am not good at running up trees.
I live in a crowd in the wild.
I eat meat and bones.

Daniel McGill (8)
Overfields Primary School, Middlesbrough

Cat - Kennings

A bird liker
A mouse hunter
A comb lover
A pole scratcher
An athletic runner
A ball lover
A carton dragger.

Connor Attwood (8)
Overfields Primary School, Middlesbrough

Snake

Call me Slow Slider.
I live in a tree because I like to spy on my food.
I have a pattern on my back and a red tongue
You can call me Slithering Snake.
I have been looking for my food all night.
I am camouflaged in the grass.
I am tired of chasing my food.
I eat white mice and bird eggs.
Do you like the pattern on my back?
You can call me Stripy Scales.
I can climb trees, but people say I can't.

Emily James (8)
Overfields Primary School, Middlesbrough

Shark - Kennings

Heart beater
Fish scraper
Water gobbler
Teeth scraper
Fin flyer
Animal eater
Blood drinker
Food taker
I am a shark.

Liam Clark (7)
Overfields Primary School, Middlesbrough

Call Me High Flyer

Call me high flyer night rider.
I live in a cave full of darkness
Because it is wet and cool.
I have jet-black wings,
And sharp fangs.
I have been hungry all day.
I eat furry mice and juicy bugs.
Do you like my dark cape?
You can call me the caped crusader.

Martin Marshall-Ellwood (9)
Overfields Primary School, Middlesbrough

I Sit On A Twig

I sit on a twig
Ready to fly on fluttering wings.
Jumping into wind from this twig.
The twig of a branch.
The branch of a tree.
The tree in the wood.
A windy wood in Overfields.

Charley Massey (7)
Overfields Primary School, Middlesbrough

Woodland

Children and animals meet in the woodland.
Worms are in the ground,
I can't see them.
The trees and plants have died during the winter.
The trees and plants will grow in the spring.

Liam Bivens (10)
Overfields Primary School, Middlesbrough

Call Me Squirmy Sausage

Call me squirmy sausage.
I live in crunchy leaves
Because leaves are my tea.
I am the hungry consumer.
I have mini spikes and a jelly belly.
You can call me Mr Squirmy!
I am waiting until I am fat enough to spin a silky sleeping bag.
Do you like my slow movements?
I have to keep out of sight.
I want to turn into a butterfly . . .
I can't wait to have all the blues and yellows like a flower.

Tiegan Helm (8)
Overfields Primary School, Middlesbrough

Little Miss Beauty

Little Red Riding Hood also known as Beauty
She's so sweet; everyone thinks she's a cutie.

With lots of goodies off to Granny's she will go
Skipping through the woods, ever so slow.

Beauty stops and eats the feast
The wolf sees her and thinks she's a beast.

Meanwhile Granny's starving in bed
All cold and hungry, she hasn't been fed.

On her way, Wolfie shouts
Beauty turns round and knocks him out.

Wolfie's on the floor in fear
The woodcutter comes and says, 'Come here!'

Wolfie gets up and runs about
Then gets to Granny's and she shouts,

'You're my hero, you saved the day
Beauty, you're grounded until May!'

Amy Green (10)
Overfields Primary School, Middlesbrough

Cutie In A Hoody

Little Red Riding Hood aka Cutie in a Hoody
Sweet and kind, a real goody, goody.

She eats the sweet food every day
Just the fairy cakes, healthy fruits she tosses them away.

Is Wolfie a cowardly, cowardly chicken?
Silently spies and thinks Cutie's the queen of trickin'.

Granny at home lay on her bed
Thinking of her chicken leg.

Wolfie to the rescue, in a heartbeat
Got to stop Granny from eating her feet.

Woodcutter gets the wrong idea
Gives Wolfie a clip round the ear.

Granny stops the angry woodcutter
'Leave Wolfie alone you crazy nutter!

This wolf's my hero, he saved me in time
It's that Cutie is a hoody, who's done the crime.

From now on she'll do service in the wood
To make sure she knows bad from good.'

Jessica Mehnert (10)
Overfields Primary School, Middlesbrough

Goody Of The Wood

Little Red Riding Hood aka Goody of the Wood
Always wearing her big red hood.
Mother says, 'Off to granny's honey
It's time to deliver Gran's food and money.'
She ate all the cakes halfway there,
Left all the fruit to rot, she didn't care.
In the bushes, something's there
It's Wolfie, so easy to scare.
Meanwhile deep, deep in the woods
Granny lay hungry for her goods.
Wolfie decides to stop Goody's greed
He must help Granny, she's in need.
He runs to granny's house and just in time
And saves her life from a terrible crime.
To teach Goody (her) a lesson, she'll have to be your slave
Then she might learn how to behave.

Amber Sheridan (10)
Overfields Primary School, Middlesbrough

Cutie In Red

Little Red Riding Hood known as Cutie
Was really intelligent, took her mother's beauty.
Baking and making Granny's meal
Given a fiver was the deal.
She smelt the food, she took a peep
No one will notice, she began to eat.
What the wolf saw was a sight
Poor old Granny, is she alright?
He ran to the cottage as fast as he could
The wolf entered the room, petrified he stood.
The sight not pretty, nor was it right
With great courage and all his might,
He got out his claws ready to stab
Chopped up the lobster and the crooked crab.
'Wolfie you're a hero, thanks a lot
My granddaughter will not be queen of this plot.'

Georgia Cox (11)
Overfields Primary School, Middlesbrough

Behind These Magic Doors

I opened the sticky caramel door and saw . . .
A beautiful caramel fountain
Trickling down the fudge mountain.

I opened the golden dazzling door and saw . . .
A pile of gold sparkling in the sun
I think the caramel door was much more fun.

I opened the dream door and saw . . .
All my dreams whizzing round the room
I hope all my dreams come true very soon.
I'm coming to the end of the magic doors
But there's one last door I want to explore.
It's a dazzling, wonderful door
It's glittering, sparkling and nothing else more.

Rachel Ramsay (11)
Robert Ferguson Primary School, Carlisle

Night

Night is a dark kind time.
When he moves he moves swiftly.
When he speaks he whispers and hisses.
His face looks dark and crooked.
His eyes are shady and closed.
His mouth is small and scrunched up.
His hair is gloomy, long and grey.
His clothes are like grey rags.
He makes me comfortable and relaxed.
He lives in a dark gloomy forest with trees all around him and dark
                                                            sky above him.

Night likes me and I like him.
Good night.

Kelsey Davidson (11)
Robert Ferguson Primary School, Carlisle

Hide-And-Seek

H ere I am, come and find me
I 'm behind the tree
D ay and night
E veryone can't see me.

A nd you can't seek me
N ow I'm in the shed
D own in the garden, covered with leaves.

S ee me, seek me, you can't do it
E veryone's quiet, nothing to be seen
E veryone distant, you still haven't found me
K eep on hiding.

Nicola Nunn (10)
Robert Ferguson Primary School, Carlisle

I Saw . . .

I opened a white door and saw . . .
A football changing room full of mighty players,
A mouldy witch with a cat and broom,
A rusty skeleton almost snapped.

I opened a shiny door and saw . . .
A great white shark ready to kill,
A wrestler champion ready to fight,
A cheetah ready for a race,
That's what was behind those two doors.

Bradley Miller (11)
Robert Ferguson Primary School, Carlisle

The Writer Of This Poem

(Based on 'The Writer of This Poem' by Roger McGough)

The writer of this poem
Is as tall as a tree,
As quick as a monkey,
As tricky as a bee.

The writer of this poem
Is as light as a pancake,
As bright as a flower,
As skinny as a rake.

Leanne Thomas (11)
Robert Ferguson Primary School, Carlisle

The Headteacher's Door

I'm staring at a spooky door,
I'm scared and full of fear,
I don't want to go in,
People go in, they never come out,
I can't go in here!

This door isn't ordinary,
I'm not sure that it's real,
I reach out to touch the doorknob
I think it's made of steel.

I'm scared out of my wits,
Come take me away,
Take me to a castle,
Take me there today.

I hear a booming voice say,
'Come in here *now!*'
Goodbye everybody
I'm never coming out now!

Samantha Robson (11)
Robert Ferguson Primary School, Carlisle

The Head's Door

I sat staring,
I was scared to go in,
I wished I was in the classroom
The door was a horrible thing.

It was big, black and ugly,
I paced up and down the floor,
My face was gobsmacked,
Shock! Horror!
I was going to the headmaster's door!

Chloe Brown (11)
Robert Ferguson Primary School, Carlisle

If Only It Wasn't True

If only it wasn't true
I wouldn't feel this blue.

Why is it me
When it shouldn't be?

If only it wasn't true
I wouldn't feel this blue.

I won't tell you what it is
Or will I . . . ?

This is what's making me blue
It's because I lost my precious shoe!

Hannah Gill (10)
Robert Ferguson Primary School, Carlisle

Where Do All The Laptops Go?

Where do all the laptops go
When it's time for bed?
Do they go to PC World
And do they eat our bread?

Do they wash their microchips
And do they play my games?
But do they erase their memories
Like we forget our names!

Steffan James (11)
Robert Ferguson Primary School, Carlisle

Night Kills My Confidence

When night moves he slithers along the corridors
And covers me in a cold blanket,
When his voice speaks it comes out as a scream.
Night is an evil and haunted person.
His arms and legs are made of broken twigs and branches.
He lives in a dark forest with wolves and foxes.
His eyes are two moons faded behind the grey clouds.
His mouth is an upside-down smile.
His hair is black and thick.
His clothes are made of dark black rags.
He makes me feel scared and frightened.
Night kills my confidence!

Sally Metcalfe (11)
Robert Ferguson Primary School, Carlisle

If Only I

If only I could fly and swoop down to America at night.
If only I was invisible and could spy on people I didn't like.
If only I was a shape shifter and could creep around the house
                                        sneaking Mum's chocolates.
If only I was as fast as a cheetah and won every race.
If only I had tons of money and had all the games in the world.
If only I had everything I ever dreamed of, because that would
                                        be the best!

Jenna Selen (10)
Robert Ferguson Primary School, Carlisle

The Boogie Rap

Music beating on,
Everyone's face.
And I'm trying to
Keep the booming pace.
Party food everywhere
So I ate a flying pear,
Big black stage
On the floor
With a few
Hanging doors.
Tig is my favourite game
So I tame my fame
So this is the end of my boogie rap
See ya soon, in a little tap.

Adam Martin (11)
Robert Ferguson Primary School, Carlisle

My Dreams

I dream of floating on a cloud way up high,
And I dream of riding on a bird and soaring in the sky.
I dream of being an animal like a dog or a cat.
I dream of being a vampire and turning into a bat.
I dream of being a lamb and being able to prance and dance.
If only my dreams would give me a chance.

Bethany Hindmarsh (10)
Robert Ferguson Primary School, Carlisle

The Writer Of This Poem

(Based on 'The Writer of This Poem' by Roger McGough)

The writer of this poem
Is as fast as a streak of lightning,
As quick as a fox,
As beautiful as Goldilocks.

As bright as a genius,
As hot as a sun,
As pointed as an arrow,
As yummy as a cream bun.

Damian Childs (10)
Robert Ferguson Primary School, Carlisle

My Dream

If only I could glide to and fro across our world,
Get dropped off at Cardiff,
Stay there till there was a football match,
Actually be in the game,
Meet my hero Rachel Yankee,
Fab!
Score a wicked goal,
Get a football scholarship,
Be a footy heroine,
Win in a final,
That's my dream.

Abbie Turner (10)
Robert Ferguson Primary School, Carlisle

I Wish . . .

I wish upon a star
I wish I was on cloud nine
I wish I could go to Majorca
And live there all my life.

I wish . . .
I wish . . .
I wish upon a star.

I wish I could own a shoe shop
And I would wear them all.
I wish I could sing
And sing to my favourite songs.

I wish . . .
I wish . . .
I wish upon a star.

Lisa Annall (11)
Robert Ferguson Primary School, Carlisle

What's Behind The Door?

I opened a shiny tartan door and saw . . .
A very embarrassed teacher wearing a kilt and playing the bagpipes.
I opened a wrecked door and saw . . .
Dirty broken bones and cobwebs and spiders.
I fell down a trap door and saw . . .
A skeleton hanging on a long piece of rope and me on my bum.
I opened a sparkling glass door and saw . . .
A beautiful garden with snowdrops, roses and butterflies.
I opened a wooden door with a golden strip on it and saw . . .
The *headmaster!*

Abby Jardine (10)
Robert Ferguson Primary School, Carlisle

Laughter

Laughter is a giggle, a great joke,
An explosion,
A *ha, ha, ha!*
Laughter is a smirk,
A little whistle,
A shout out.
Laughter is an interruption,
A roar out loud,
A cackle,
Laughter is a pinch of fun!

Lauren Little (11)
Robert Ferguson Primary School, Carlisle

Darkness

Darkness feels like a dark shadow is following you.
It smells like you've been waiting in a long queue
And tastes like hunger too.
Darkness is like a dark scary tunnel.
Darkness reminds me of sweet revenge.

Connor Redden (9)
St Paul's RC Primary School, Billingham

Silence

Silence is colourless, ongoing and dull.
It smells of nothing, nothing at all.
Silence is quite calm and quiet like the waves on a lifeless sea.
Working in silence is hard to do, it's depressing like silence.
It tastes of very dry air.
It reminds me of nothing, nothing but silence.

Anna Fairs (11)
St Paul's RC Primary School, Billingham

Happiness

Happiness is the colour of white.
It sounds like the bell of Heaven.
It feels like the warmth of the sun.
It smells like the scent of red roses in bloom.
It tastes like the love in your hearts.
It reminds me of fun.

Abigail Noble (10)
St Paul's RC Primary School, Billingham

Fun

Fun is blue like happiness.
It smells like ice cream on a beach.
Fun tastes like fries.
It feels like a treat.
Fun is happiness.

Andrew Wilson (9)
St Paul's RC Primary School, Billingham

Fun

Fun is blue like the midday sky with no clouds in it.
It sounds like air whistling away
And tastes like small drops of rain landing in your mouth.
It smells light and bright like the smell of a barbecue
And feels like walking through water.
Fun reminds me of light green grass.

James McCabe (10)
St Paul's RC Primary School, Billingham

Darkness

Darkness is black, like being deserted in a forest at night
And sounds like silence in a deserted house.
It tastes like air in a pitch-black cupboard with no window
It smells like a graveyard in darkness
And feels like someone creeping behind you about to kill.
Darkness reminds me of lying in bed, when it's dark and lonely.

Lauriane Povey (10)
St Paul's RC Primary School, Billingham

Love

Love is the colour pink,
It sounds like a hosepipe with a kink.
It feels so silky,
It sounds like the droplets of milk.
It tastes so sweet,
It reminds me of hugs and kisses.

Jennifer Robinson (10)
St Paul's RC Primary School, Billingham

Sadness

Sadness is blue, like a tear of a person.
It sounds like a baby's cry
And tastes like a freezing ice block.
It smells of nothing, like water
And feels like swimming in freezing water.
Sadness reminds me of a sad person crying.

Joseph Armstrong (9)
St Paul's RC Primary School, Billingham

Silence

Silence is grey, like a snowy day.
It sounds like a pin dropping a mile away.
It tastes like a waterfall down your throat
And smells like fresh air in the middle of May.
It's like walking on solid concrete.
It reminds me of walking down a deserted street.

Hannah McLaren (9)
St Paul's RC Primary School, Billingham

Happiness

Happiness is yellow like a hot summer's day
And it sounds like sweet hummingbirds singing together.
It tastes like sweet tasting chocolate
And smells strong like pinewood from a forest.
It feels like swinging gently in a park.
Happiness reminds me of the happiness on a great holiday.

Liam Taylor (10)
St Paul's RC Primary School, Billingham

Love

Love is red, like a cherry tomato in the shape of a heart
And sounds like romantic music.
It tastes like chocolate and caramel.
It smells like melting sugar
And feels like a gentle massage.
Love reminds me of a soothing jacuzzi.

Ryan Branley (10)
St Paul's RC Primary School, Billingham

Hunger

Hunger is brown like an empty stomach.
It can't be heard like a very dark noiseless night.
It feels empty like a street at night.
It can't be smelt like the air.
It tastes of nothing but horrible hunger.
It reminds me of nobody, of nothing near me, nothing left.

Louis Kelly (10)
St Paul's RC Primary School, Billingham

Happiness

Happiness is blue like the sea slowly moving.
It sounds like two bluebirds singing sweetly in the morning
And it tastes like fresh fruit straight from the ground.
It smells like a sweet aroma.
It feels like the softest silk in the world.
It reminds me of my loving family.

Hope Cain (10)
St Paul's RC Primary School, Billingham

Silence

Silence is the colour of snowy mountains.
It sounds like the wind blowing you along
And it tastes like melted candyfloss.
It smells like the sweet smell of outdoors
And feels like a silk sheet.
Silence reminds me of lying under the stars at night.

Susie Walls (10)
St Paul's RC Primary School, Billingham

Fun

Fun is like the colour yellow like the sun.
Fun is like a hot summer's day.
Fun sounds like the waves splashing around with kids in it.
Fun tastes like cool ice cream on your lips.
Fun smells like suntan lotion.
Fun feels like the hot sandy beach.
Fun reminds me of a hot day at the beach.

Catherine Menzies (9)
St Paul's RC Primary School, Billingham

Hunger

Hunger is brown, like crumbs of bread
Dripping from the hairs on his head.
It sounds like bubbles all around and glowing all around
And tastes like trying to find no food, drink, not even a blink.
It feels like a crust not eating anywhere.
And it feels like fasting for nine days and no work to pay.
Hunger reminds me of starving all day long and not even singing a
song.

Omer Siddiqui (9)
St Paul's RC Primary School, Billingham

A Winter Poem

When the winter starts
The children wrap up warm.
The children playing snowball fights.
All the flowers popped their heads into the white ground.
The snow covering streets and Christmas is nearly here.
They all get ready for spring is nearly ready to show its blossom.
The lovely pink and red colours are here.
The spring has started.

Alexa Singleton (7)
The Avenue Primary School, Middlesbrough

Flowers

Flowers by day and flowers by night
How do you see, it's so bright?

Big coloured petals for all to see
Lots of pollen for the honeybee.

Large green stem to hold them high
To soak up the sun high in the sky.

They smell so sweet, gorgeous too
I think it's good, how about you?

Molly Ryan (7)
The Avenue Primary School, Middlesbrough

My Teddy Bear

My teddy bear
Sits on my chair
He's soft and cute
And plays the flute.

His twinkly brown eyes
Are a very big size
And his cute button nose
Can balance a rose.

I love my bear
And he loves me
When we're together
We're as happy as can be.

Hannah Marshall (8)
The Avenue Primary School, Middlesbrough

Nonsense, Nonsense!

When the days were cold
And the nights were old
And the donkeys all ate ships.
They sailed the seas in aeroplanes
And flew around on chips!

These days most cats
Wear fancy hats
All covered in feathery slime.
While dogs chew TV in pyjamas
And fish can tell the time!

Folks all play the fiddledoo
Whilst riding on a kangaroo
And snoring in a glass.
Teachers write on apple trees
And always eat their class!

Matthew Bennison (9)
The Avenue Primary School, Middlesbrough

Moving House With Puppies

Puppies, puppies everywhere!
Puppies don't know where to stare.

No don't help, undo that box
You can come over, the gobbly fox.

You can't dance there, that's all my things for my hair
I need to sell them at the car boot fair.

No, you can't play football in that room
Otherwise the ball will go *bazoom!*

Why not go and unpack your stuff?
That's where you can play footy!

Philippa Stone (7)
The Avenue Primary School, Middlesbrough

Morning And Night

The shops all open
In the morning dawn
Mrs Pecking Pigeon
Was pecking on the lawn.

The cars are all tooting
Cos the lights are on red
The drivers are grumpy
Because they had to get out of bed.

The lollypop lady
Is happy and jolly
The school kids are safe
Cos they cross with the lolly.

Night-time is coming
It's been a lovely day
Children cuddle up fast asleep
Tired from their play.

Lucy Chambers (8)
The Avenue Primary School, Middlesbrough

My Cat

I have a cat
I called her Buffy
She lies on the mat
Always looking fluffy.

She loves her food
If she does not get any
It puts her in a mood
She is really canny.

I will love her forever
She loves me too
I will keep her forever
My mum and dad love her too.

Alexandra Pinyoun (7)
The Avenue Primary School, Middlesbrough

A Season Full Of Surprises

In spring the leaves come back and make the world look nice,
Soon the blossom on the trees look pink and rosy.
A gust of wind may soon pass by, but journeys are still to come,
Now there's Easter to enjoy.

In summer the sun shines bright, beaches are in sight.
The colours of the sunny sky shine high up in the sky.
The flowers droop beneath the hot sun, waiting for the rain to come.

In autumn the crispy leaves fall off the trees and the wind is
blowing wild,
Let's wrap up warm all through till dawn, till the farmers harvest
the corn.

In wintertime the snowflakes float down from the sky,
The icicles form above.
Children are having fun throwing snowballs.
The fire is on; we're nice and warm, Christmas will soon come.

Rebecca Moy (7)
The Avenue Primary School, Middlesbrough

The Summer Wind

The summer wind is a fairy sneeze,
It strokes the petals on the flowers,
The flowers seem to throb and smile,
The flowers seem to thrive in the summer wind.

Lauren Baxter (10)
The Avenue Primary School, Middlesbrough

A Monstrous Storm

Thunder roars like a lion
The wind thrusts itself upon me,
A tornado twirls in fear.
Why is this happening to me?
Where is my family?
I'm sat in darkness, all alone.
All I can feel is trembling and fear in my bones.
As the storm gets bigger, it starts to roar and groan.
Should I run, should I hide?
What am I to do?
Only I know, and I mean only I know.
It is the start of a monstrous storm.

Hannah Dring (9)
The Avenue Primary School, Middlesbrough

People Of A Summer's Sunset

People of a summer sunset,
A red is a good fellow
And the orange always bellows
While the yellow says hello
And together they are one
Joyful and mellow.

Red is for people
Who always lay in bed,
Red is for people
Who can always raise their head.
Red is for a person
Who is a good friend.
Red is for people
On whom you can always depend.

Orange is for people
Who like to be free.
Orange is for people
Who can't disagree.
Orange is for people
Who are willing to give.
Orange is for people
Who love to live.

Yellow is for people
Who like to dream.
Yellow is for people
Who like chocolate and ice cream.
Yellow is for people
Who are happy and fun.
Yellow is for people
Who like to play under the hot summer sun.

We're all people of the summer sunset
You, me, him and her
And in the coldest of times
Happiness we'll stir!

Smarika Tuladhar (10)
The Avenue Primary School, Middlesbrough

Giraffes In Hollywood

Giraffes, giraffes, giraffes,
Some are smart and have a knack for art.

Giraffes, giraffes, giraffes,
Some are weird and are growing a beard.

Giraffes, giraffes, giraffes,
Some are crazy and so, so lazy!

Giraffes, giraffes, giraffes,
Some are giggly and so wriggly!

Giraffes, giraffes, giraffes,
Some are too cool for school.

One of each is better and are friends forever
These giraffes are friends to the end.

Abbie Carroll (9)
The Avenue Primary School, Middlesbrough

Dogs

Some are sweet
Some like meat
And some will even bite your feet.

Some bark
Some like the dark
If they're called Mark.

Some are fat
Some are thin
If they go on races and win.

Natasha Hart (9)
The Avenue Primary School, Middlesbrough

The House That Is Next To Mine

The house that is next to mine
Is spooky indeed
With a squeaky door
And ragged walls
That is the house that is next to mine.

The house that is next to mine
Is spooky indeed
With dirty windows
And creaking stairs
That is the house that is next to mine.

The house that is next to mine
Is spooky indeed
With falling tiles
And smoking chimneys
That is the house that is next to mine.

Adam Gamesby (9)
The Avenue Primary School, Middlesbrough

When I Was Off School With My Cough . . .

When I was off school with my cough . . .
I did like cuddling my dad.
I didn't like feeling so bad.

When I was off school with my cough . . .
I did like missing numeracy,
I didn't like missing literacy.

When I was off school with my cough . . .
I did like listening to music really loud,
I didn't miss my teacher shouting out loud.

When I was off school with my cough . . .
I did like watching TV
I didn't like being sick, all over the settee.

Lauren Riddel (7)
The Avenue Primary School, Middlesbrough

All The Animals

P arrots copy everything you say
E lectric eels light up in the bay
T ortoises go as slow as snails
S lugs leave slimy trails.

Charlie Munkley (10)
The Avenue Primary School, Middlesbrough

Sounds

The brilliant blue sways above my eyes
Green spikes brush past my legs
Whilst the traffic and birds bounce
The sound of people rushing past fills my ears
As well as the wind.

Sona Singh (10)
The Avenue Primary School, Middlesbrough

A Country Animal

It has floppy ears
And a fluffy tail,
It nibbles on carrots
And lives in a burrow
Wagging its tail.

Richard Michael Goldsbrough (10)
The Avenue Primary School, Middlesbrough

Life

Life is nice, life is tough
Sometimes nice, sometimes rough.
Full of joy, full of strife
That is the recipe of life.
Use it right or it will go wrong
Because you will not get along.

Michael Benson (10)
The Avenue Primary School, Middlesbrough

Dream

I lay in my bed
As though I were dead.
I shut my eyes
And fill my world with lies.
Tap, tap, tap.
What was that?
I picture a wild cat
Suddenly everything's changed
I know what I've gained
My dream!

Priyanki Nirmal (10)
The Avenue Primary School, Middlesbrough

Molly The Miracle

Molly is a miracle
A gift sent from God
If only she didn't chew the bait
On the fishing rod!
Molly can't be real
She's too good to be real,
So what's the explanation for this soft fur I feel?

I gaze into her hypnotising eyes
And envy her shiny black coat,
Molly is way too gentle
To scratch me on the throat!
When I stare into her eyes, I get a big surprise
As fun and joy bounces around in the middle of her pupils,
Molly loves me and I love her too,
Wouldn't you?

Lucy Aitken (9)
The Avenue Primary School, Middlesbrough

Where's My Sock?

I can't find my sock today,
I looked on the chair but I couldn't find it there.
On the kitchen floor and by the utility door.
I looked in the cupboard under the stairs
But I still couldn't find it anywhere.
So then I went upstairs and looked on the wooden stairs,
It wasn't there!
I started to get a bit worried because I couldn't find my lucky sock
anywhere.
A minute later my mum called me down to the utility room,
My sock had been in the washing machine without its pair.

Rebecca Watson (11)
Welton Primary School, Welton

Lions

I went to Africa and I saw lions in a pride
And if they looked at me I would run and hide.
I liked to watch them lying in the summer sun
With the cubs around them running.
A cub learns to hunt from dawn till dusk,
A cub gets stuck in a bush
I like watching lion cubs because they're very, very cute.
I like to watch the big lions because
They look very, very soft, cuddly and fluffy.

Olivia Caldwell (7)
Welton Primary School, Welton

Questions

(For my grandpa who died on 30th January, 2006)

Can it be frosty with a cloudy sky?
Can it be warm when the sun is not high?
Can you understand if the words are not clear?
Can you be missed even though you are not here?

Can we do things that we have not learnt?
Can we have money that we have not earned?
Can there be stones on a sandy beach?
Can there be too much if there's more than one each?

Questions are asked by boy and by girl
Questions are asked by old and by young
Each one is their own
And each one will be done.

Emily Green (11)
Welton Primary School, Welton

Donkey

Ee-or, ee-or
That's what donkey says
Ee-or, ee-or
He wants to play.
He's on the beach
Hooray, hooray.
He's in the field
That is where he likes to stay.
He's had a hard day
So, come to tea
We want to play
Just you and me.

Sarah Wolstencroft (8)
Welton Primary School, Welton

My Star Wars Poem

Star Wars films are fantastic; the aliens are so real
I think they may be made of plastic!
Greedo with his beady eyes and big hands their size does not match.
I bet if a ball whizzed past he could make the perfect catch!
At Jabbar's palace music is the scene
Max Rebo's floppy ears catch everyone's attention.
Especially as they are coloured bright blue
When playing music right on cue.
They are so cool, they make a tremendous team
His red ball organ can be heard in far-off galaxies
The best you have ever seen.

Sam Mead (8)
Welton Primary School, Welton

Where's Teddy?

My teddy had gone missing today and I didn't know where he was.
I looked upstairs in my bedroom and he wasn't there.
I looked in my wardrobe and in the airing cupboard and I still could
not find him.
I looked in the colourful bathroom and I thought I'd better go and
look downstairs.
I looked under the sofa and under the stairs, but I still couldn't
find him anywhere.
I looked under my computer desk and on my computer chair and
I couldn't find him there.
So I decided to go back upstairs and I looked under my pink bedcover
and he was there!

Megan Wetherell (9)
Welton Primary School, Welton

I Know Someone Who Can

I know someone who can . . .
Hop across the playground.
I know someone who can . . .
Ride a pony.
I know someone who can . . .
Run very fast.
I know someone who can . . .
Jump very high.
I know someone who can . . .
Be very brave at the dentist
And that someone is me!

Chloe Watson (8)
Welton Primary School, Welton

The Globe

The globe is a wonderful thing
It has Italy, Pakistan, France, Wales and everywhere else
But it does not have my world.
My world is a wonderful place
Lions are kings and that's just the start of things.
The river is pink, the sky is red, the grass is yellow
And then I wake up
And find it's a dream
I am sad but I am glad for what I have seen.

Sophie Rheam   (9)
Welton Primary School, Welton

I Know Someone Who Can

I know someone who can do her work right.
I know someone who can read in her head.
I know someone who can sing the alphabet when riding her bike.
I know someone who can tidy her room in ten minutes.
I know someone who can write really good stories at school.
I know someone who can swing upside down on a bar when being
                                                watched by lots of people

And that happy person is me!

Catherine Stobart (9)
Welton Primary School, Welton